Presented to

_____

On the occasion of

_____

From

_____

Date

_____

The One I Love

Inspirational Thoughts on Love and Devotion

Ellyn Sanna

BARBOUR
PUBLISHING, INC.

©MCMXCIX by Barbour Publishing, Inc.

ISBN 1-57748-538-6

Published by Barbour Publishing, Inc., P.O. Box 719, Uhrichsville, Ohio 44683 http://www.barbourbooks.com

Member of the
Evangelical Christian
Publishers Association

Printed in China.

Contents

White Lace and Promises:
The Beginning of the Road

Place me like a seal over your heart,
like a seal on your arm;
for love is as strong as death. . . .
It burns like blazing fire,
like a mighty flame.
SONG OF SOLOMON 8:6 (NIV)

My heart is like a singing bird
    Whose nest is in a watered shoot;
My heart is like an apple-tree
    Whose boughs are bent with thick-set fruit;
My heart is like a rainbow shell
    That paddles in a halcyon sea;
My heart is gladder than all these,
    Because my love is come to me.
        —CHRISTINA GEORGINA ROSSETTI

Many waters cannot quench love;
rivers cannot wash it away.
SONG OF SOLOMON 8:7 (NIV)

Marriage is a road we walk, around bends and up hills, through delightful valleys and across long deserts. Our wedding day is the gate by which we enter this long and lovely road. We cannot know where this road will lead, for we cannot know the future. But our faith in one another makes us step out unafraid.

And we do not walk alone along this road, for Christ goes with us all the way.

How can we be troubled about the future road, since it belongs to Thee? How can we be troubled where it leads, since it finally but leads us to Thee?

—JOHN HENRY NEWMAN

Love me for love's sake, that evermore
Thou may'st love on through love's eternity.
—ELIZABETH BARRETT BROWNING

10 Romantic Places to Go with the One I Love

1. A quaint bed-and-breakfast in the middle of nowhere (the library will have a directory)
2. A four-star hotel in the center of a big city (like the Plaza in New York)
3. A long, empty beach (like Plum Island in Massachusetts or the Outer Banks in North Carolina)
4. A ski lodge in Vermont or Colorado
5. A cabin in the woods (a state park, maybe)
6. An ocean cruise (freighters are just as romantic and cost less)
7. Somewhere that time's stood still (like Williamsburg, Virginia or Quebec City in Canada)
8. Paris (let's go ahead and dream—anything's possible)
9. Niagara Falls (the traditional spot for honeymooners)
10. Anywhere the two of us can spend time alone

I will make you brooches and toys for your delight
Of bird-song at morning and star-shine at night.
I will make a palace fit for you and me,
Of green days in forests and blue days at sea.
—ROBERT LOUIS STEVENSON

Love Letter
from John Keats to Fanny Brawne, 1818

I must write you a line or two and see if that will assist in dismissing you from my mind for ever so short a time. Upon my soul I can think of nothing else. . . . I am forgetful of everything but seeing you again— my life seems to stop there—I see no further. You have absorbed me. I have a sensation at the present moment as though I was dissolving— I should be exquisitely miserable without the hope of soon seeing you. I should be afraid to separate myself far from you. My sweet Fanny, will your heart never change? My love, will it? I have no limit now to my love. . . .

Lord, I am not worthy of so good a husband; but help us both to observe the holiness of wedded life, so that we may eternally abide together near Thee.

—ELIZABETH OF HUNGARY, 1207–1231

Doubt that the stars are fire;
  Doubt that the sun doth move,
Doubt truth to be a liar;
  But never doubt I love.
    —WILLIAM SHAKESPEARE, *Hamlet*

Love Letter
from Henry Preston to his wife, Mary, 1924

Dear one, my heart feels as though it might burst with joy, so glad I am to be one with you. You lie there sleeping, just three feet from my chair, and I can scarce believe you're real. Perhaps I'll wake soon and find that you and all we've shared are just a pretty dream.

But no, I stretch out my hand and touch you, feel you warm and solid. Thank God, thank God.

I promise, my love, to be true to you always. I know this is just the beginning of our life; I know we cannot know what will come next, a year down the road, ten years, fifty years. But I trust the future to God, to you, to our love. Whatever comes, I will only love you more.

I picked up this pen only to write a note to say—I've gone out for coffee and rolls. If you wake and find me gone, I shall be back immediately. But once I put the pen to paper, I found I could not keep the words of love from rolling out of me, like a river at springtime filled to overflowing with water.

That is how I feel, filled to overflowing with love and life, and all because of you. But if one day, the river should run dry, still, my love, believe me: I will be true.

Love should be essentially an act of the will. . . . It is a decision. . . . It is a promise.

—ERICH FROMM

Dear God, as we begin our married life together, please be present with us. We ask You to help us keep the promises we've made to one another. Thank You for the joy and love You've given us. May Your Spirit always be with us. Amen.

For you have heard my vows, O God. . . .
Then will I ever sing praise to your name
and fulfill my vows day after day.
PSALM 61:5, 8 (NIV)

Forever Lovers:
Two Paths Join and Become One

Kiss me again and again, for your love is sweeter than wine.
SONG OF SONGS 1:2 (NLT)

Love's mysteries in souls do grow
And yet the body is his book.
—JOHN DONNE

10 Ways to Say "I Love You"

1. Surprise your love with flowers
2. Put it in writing
3. Schedule a get-away weekend for the two of you
4. Listen to the other person's dreams
5. Surprise your spouse by going out and getting a little piece of those dreams
6. Make a habit of saying the words "I Love You" every chance you get

7.   Serve your love's favorite foods
8.   Take a nap together
9.   Do each other's chores
10. Pay attention to the things that please your love the most—
     and then do them!

How do I love thee? Let me count the ways.
   I love thee to the depth and breadth and height
My soul can reach, when feeling out of sight
   For the ends of Being and ideal Grace.
I love thee to the level of every day's
   Most quiet need, by sun and candlelight.
I love thee freely, as men strive for Right;
   I love thee purely, as men turn from Praise.
I love thee with the passion put to use
   In my old griefs, and with my childhood's faith.
I love thee with a love I seemed to lose
   With my lost saints,—I love thee with the breath,
Smiles, tears, of all my life!—and, if God choose,
   I shall but love thee better after death.
                    —ELIZABETH BARRETT BROWNING

It is a fusion of two hearts—the union of two lives—the coming together of two tributaries, which after being joined in marriage, will flow in the same channel in the same direction. . .carrying the same burdens of responsibility and obligation.

—PETER MARSHALL

Characteristic of love is its *tenderness*. . . . In love hands don't take, grasp or hold. They caress. Caressing is the possibility of human hands to be tender. The careful touch of the hand makes for growth. Like a gardener who carefully touches the flowers to enable the light to shine through and stimulate growth, the hand of the lover allows for the full self-expression of the other. In love the mouth does not bite, devour or destroy. It kisses.

—HENRI J. M. NOUWEN, *Intimacy*

And what is a kiss when all is done?
A rosy dot over the "i" of loving.
—EDMUND ROSTAND,
Cyrano de Bergerac

Love Letter
from Anne Bradstreet to her husband, 1678

If ever two were one, then surely we.
    If ever man were loved by wife, then thee;
If ever wife was happy in a man,
    Compare with ye women if you can.
I prize thy love more than whole mines of gold,
    Or all the riches that the East doth hold.
My love is such that rivers cannot quench,
    Nor ought but love from thee give recompense.
Thy love is such I can no way repay;
    The heavens reward thee manifold, I pray.
Then while we live, in love let's so persevere,
    That when we live no more we may love better.

Love vanquishes time. To lovers, a moment can be eternity, eternity can be the tick of a clock.

—MARY PARRISH, *All the Love in the World*

Love must be learned, and learned again and again; there is no end to it.

—KATHERINE ANNE PORTER

Love Letter
from Henry Preston to his wife, 1930

Dear one, remember the time on our honeymoon when we raced to see who could get to the bed first? We both jumped at the same time, and that solid wood bed collapsed under our combined weight. All these years into our marriage, I suspect we should not be surprised if our marriage bed collapses from time to time. After all, the combined weight of our two lives can become rather cumbersome. But just recall, love: We only needed laughter and patience to get our honeymoon bed back in service, and I suspect we shall find the same is true today. And who can tell? I should not be in the least surprised if the reconstructed version gives us even more pleasure and delight than it did before.

Like the sun, love radiates and warms into life all that it touches.

—O. S. MARDEN

Love is not lust, and lust is not love. Love, if it is anything at all, is respect; and when respect for the other's dignity and integrity is thrown aside, love folds up like a punctured balloon.

—BILLY GRAHAM

Only in a marriage—a marriage where love is—can sex develop into the delightfully positive force God meant it to be. Here is where the excitement of sex really is. When a man and a woman make a lifelong commitment to love and cherish each other, they are giving themselves the time they will need to dismantle the barriers of restraint, shyness, defensiveness, and selfishness that exist between all human beings. It cannot be done in a night or with a rush of passion. It takes time to know and be known.

—COLLEEN TOWNSEND EVANS, *A New Joy*

The Christian idea of marriage is based on Christ's words that a man and wife are to be regarded as a single organism—for that is what the words "one flesh" would be in modern English. And the Christians believe that when He said this He was not expressing a sentiment but stating a fact—just as one is stating a fact when one says that a lock and its key are one mechanism, or that a violin and a bow are one musical instrument. The inventor of the human machine was telling us that its two halves, the male and the female, were meant to be combined together in pairs, not simply on the sexual level, but totally combined.

—C. S. LEWIS, *Mere Christianity*

Dear God, thank You for this love You've given us, and thank You for the delight it brings to us. Thank You for this wonderful gift with which You've blessed our lives. Remind us never to take it for granted, but to give our love the care and attention we would give to anything that is precious to us. Teach us new ways to please each other so that our love may grow day by day and year by year. Amen.

Beloved, let us love one another:
for love is of God;
and every one that loveth is
born of God, and knoweth God.
1 JOHN 4:7 (KJV)

Companions on Life's Road:
Facing Life Together

Don't urge me to leave you or to turn back from you.
Where you go I will go, and where you stay I will stay.
Your people will be my people and your God my God.
Where you die I will die, and there I will be buried.
May the LORD deal with me, be it ever so severely,
if anything but death separates you and me.
RUTH 1:16–17 (NIV)

You are my companion
Down the silver road,
Still and many-changing,
Infinitely changing,
You are my companion.

Something sings in lives—
Days of walking on and on—
Deep beyond all singing,
Wonderful past singing.

This more wonderful—
We are here together,
I am your companion.
You are my companion,
My own true companion.
—EDITH FRANKLIN WYATT

Love doesn't make the world go 'round. Love is what makes the ride worthwhile.

—FRANKLIN P. JONES

The goal in marriage is not to think alike, but to think together.
—ROBERT C. DODDS

Love does not consist in gazing at each other but in looking outward together in the same direction.

—ANTOINE DE SAINT-EXUPÉRY

Married life. . .isn't a time for settling down but for growth, for doing new things. With each passing year a growing couple will actively look for new and different things they can do together.
—DALE EVANS ROGERS, *God in the Hard Times*

Love Letter
from Napoleon Bonaparte to Josephine, 1810

My one and only Josephine, apart from you there is no joy; away from you the world is a desert where I am alone and cannot open my heart. You have taken more than my soul; you are the one thought of my life. When I am tired of the worry of work, when I fear the outcome, when men annoy me. . .I put my hand on my heart; your portrait hangs there, I look at it, and love brings me perfect happiness. . . . Oh, my adorable wife! I don't know what fate has in store for me, but if it keeps me apart from you any longer, it will be unbearable! My courage is not enough for that.

Come and join me; before we die let us at least be able to say: "We had so many happy days!"

We are each of us angels with only one wing. And we can only fly embracing each other.

—LUCIANO DE CRESCENZO

To have joy one must share it,—
Happiness was born a twin.
—LORD BYRON

Husband and wife must love each other unconditionally, must give each other room to grow, must wait for the infinite reaches of their personality to flower. Each must take the other by the hand along an unglimpsed road, developing the undreamed of potential of that other being. That is the power you have over each other and, in exercising it, you will know that you are one.

—LOUIS EVELY, *Lovers in Marriage*

Love Letter
from Henry Preston to his wife, 1941

My love, I feel slightly foolish confessing how much I miss you. After all, you have only been gone not quite twenty-four hours. Only now, though, do I realize how much I have come to depend upon your companionship. Going to the grocer is amusing when you are with me, chopping firewood gives me more pleasure when I know you are applauding my efforts, and all the small, household chores have meaning simply because we do them side by side.

How empty the house seemed tonight when I returned home— dark and cold and lonely. Eating my supper alone, my heart longed for your company. Oh my love, my best companion, how I miss you!

Dear God, I am so grateful You gave me a companion on my life's road. Teach us how to walk together. If one stumbles, give us strength to help the other up. When my beloved gets ahead of me, help me to hurry to catch up—and when my beloved falls behind, remind me to wait patiently until we walk hand in hand together once more. Thank You that I do not walk my road alone. Amen.

Two people can accomplish more than twice as much as one. . . .
If one person falls, the other can reach out and help.
But people who are alone when they fall are in real trouble.
And on a cold night, two under the same blanket
can gain warmth from each other.
ECCLESIASTES 4:9–11 (NLT)

Best Friends:
The Road of Intimacy

Can two people walk together without agreeing on the direction?
Amos 3:3 (NLT)

Two hearts, two lives
Joined together in friendship
United forever in love.

The Heart's Anchor

Think of me as your friend, I pray,
    And call me by a loving name;
I will not care what others say,
    If only you will remain the same.
I will not care how dark the night,
    I will not care how wild the storm,
Your love will fill my heart with light
    And shield me close and keep me warm.
—William Winter

10 Little Ways to Express
My Appreciation to the One I Love

1. Write a love note and put it in a lunch bag or suitcase
2. Serve my love breakfast in bed
3. Give my love a back rub
4. Write a love note on the bathroom mirror
5. Go see a movie I don't really want to see—but my love does
6. Surprise my love with a cold drink on a hot day—or a warm one on a cold day
7. Remember to say "thank you" for even routine chores
8. Express my appreciation for my love's physical appearance
9. Clean off the car in the winter and warm it up before my love goes to work in the morning
10. Never criticize my love to others

What a thing friendship is—
World without end!
—ROBERT BROWNING

Knowing is the most profound kind of love, giving someone the gift of knowledge about yourself.

—MARSHA NORMAN

The movement into marriage involves the risks of intimacy. In marriage I must be able to come close to you in a way that lets you know and influence me. I must face the risk of being changed, of coming to a different awareness of who I am, as a result of our life together. I must accept the responsibility of my own influence in your life as well. Intimacy involves an overlapping of space, a willingness to be influenced, an openness to the possibility of change. It invites me beyond myself.

—Evelyn and James Whitehead, *Marrying Well*

Friendship—our friendship—
is like the beautiful shadows of evening,
spreading and growing till life and its life pass away.
—Michael Vitkovics

Tenderness emerges from the fact that two persons, longing, as all individuals do, to overcome the separateness and isolation to which we are all heir because we are individuals, can participate in a relationship that, for the moment, is not of two isolated selves but a union.

—Rollo May

Love Letter
to Eldridge Cleaver, twentieth century

Believe this: I accept you. I know you little and I know you much, but whichever way it goes, I accept you. Your manhood comes through in a thousand ways, rare and wonderful. I accept you. . . .

What an awesome thing it is to feel oneself on the verge of the possibility of really knowing another person. . . . Getting to know someone, entering that new world, is an ultimate, irretrievable leap into the unknown. . . . We recognize each other. And having recognized each other, is it any wonder that our souls hold hands and cling together even while our minds equivocate, hesitate, vacillate, and tremble?

The greatest happiness of life is the conviction that we are loved, loved for ourselves, or rather loved in spite of ourselves.

—VICTOR HUGO

We can have no relationship of depth or authenticity if we insist there is nothing wrong with us, or that it is always the other person's fault. . . . To refuse to take responsibility and admit our flaws makes the intimacy and love we seek. . .an impossibility.

—REBECCA MANLEY PIPPERT, *Hope Has Its Reasons*

Dear God, thank You that my love is also my best friend. Sometimes we seem so different—and yet I know that our love and commitment to each other means that we can always count on each other, share everything, and learn from each other. Teach us to enjoy our differences and celebrate the unique qualities that make our life together always exciting, never boring. I am so grateful for this special best friend You've given me. Help me to show my love how much I appreciate the friendship we share. Amen.

> *Let us stop just saying we love each other;*
> *let us really show it by our actions.*
> 1 JOHN 3:18 (NLT)

For Better, For Worse:
Going Further Down the Road

Be humble and gentle.
Be patient with each other, making allowance for
each other's faults because of your love.
Always keep yourselves united in the Holy Spirit,
and bind yourselves together with peace.
EPHESIANS 4:2–3 (NLT)

Grow old along with me!
The best is yet to be,
The last of life, for which the first
was made.
—ROBERT BROWNING

10 Ways to Add Romance to Your Life

1. Eat with music playing
2. Light candles
3. Redecorate your bedroom

4. Take a walk in the moonlight
5. Go "parking" in the country
6. Go for a hansom cab ride
7. Rent a romantic movie and curl up together to watch it
8. Meet for lunch—and make plans for your evening
9. Rent a canoe and bring a picnic
10. Hold hands

At the top of the list [of what makes a successful marriage], I think, is a sense of humor.

—DEBORAH KERR

We don't naturally grow together and love each other more. We tend to grow apart, to grow distant. So we have to work hard at marriage. It's the most fun work in the world, but still it's work.

—ANNE ORTLUND

When two caring people who are committed to each other wrestle with the inevitable hard times that confront every married couple in the spirit of kindness and tenderness and forgiveness, miracles do happen.

—DALE EVANS ROGERS, *God in the Hard Times*

Maybe we remember the few occasions in our life in which we were able to show [the person] we love our real self: not only our great successes but also our weaknesses and pains, not only our good intentions but also our bitter motives, not only our radiant face but also our dark shadow. . . . People might call us a crazy idealist, an unrealistic dreamer, a first-class romanticist, but it does not touch us very deeply because we know with a new form of certainty which we had never experienced before that peace, forgiveness, justice, and inner freedom are more than mere words.

. . .We don't have to be afraid of every conflict and avoid every argument. It is here where love creates a smile, and where humor can be soft instead of cynical.

—HENRY J. M. NOUWEN, *Intimacy*

Trouble is a part of your life, and if you don't share it, you don't give the person who loves you enough chance to love you enough.

—DINAH SHORE

It is not true that love makes all things easy; it makes us choose what is difficult.

—GEORGE ELIOT

Love is the river of life in this world. Think not that ye know it who stand at the little tinkling rill, the first small fountain.

Not until you have gone through the rocky gorges and not lost the stream; not until you have gone through the meadow, and the stream has widened and deepened until fleets could ride on its bosom; not until beyond the meadow you have come to the unfathomable ocean, and poured your treasure into its depths—not until then can you know what love is.

—Henry Ward Beecher

Love Letter
from Bismarck to Joanna, nineteenth century

We are not united for the sake of sharing with each other only that which gives pleasure; but that you may pour out your heart at all times to me and I to you, whatever it may contain; that I must and will bear your sorrows, your thoughts, your naughtinesses, if you have any, and love you as you are—not as you ought to be or might be. Make me serviceable. . . . I am there for that purpose, at your disposal; but never be embarrassed in any way with me. Trust me unreservedly in the conviction that I accept everything that comes from you with profound love.

It is good to have a healthy honesty on the part of those married longer years, as they relate that awful moment of anger when the wedding ring was thrown on the floor and rolled into a crack and took two hours to find and put back on. It is good for the ones married just a short time to know that a marriage can weather "down" moments and rough places, as well as coming to know that it is important to work at relationships.

—EDITH SCHAEFFER, *What Is a Family?*

Disregarding another person's faults preserves love.
PROVERBS 17:9 (NLT)

But love is a durable fire
    In the mind ever burning;
Never sick, never old, never dead,
    From itself never turning.
        —SIR WALTER RALEIGH

Dear God, thank You that You have given us a love that will stand the test of time. We intend to keep our promises to each other, no matter what; we know You will give us the strength to walk our marriage path from beginning to end. Thank You for the joy and laughter, passion and intimacy we have found in our marriage— and thank You, too, for the heartaches and hurt feelings, the arguments and conflicts. Through it all, may we keep our eyes on You, so that our commitment to each other will grow stronger and deeper, a "durable fire" that will never be extinguished.

They are like trees planted along the riverbank,
bearing fruit each season without fail.
Their leaves never wither,
and in all they do, they prosper.
For the LORD watches over the path of the godly.
PSALM 1:3, 6 (NLT)

True Love
Wears God's Face:
Loving as God Loves

Love is patient and kind.
Love is not jealous or boastful or proud or rude.
Love does not demand its own way.
Love is not irritable, and it keeps no record
of when it has been wronged.
It is never glad about injustice but
rejoices whenever the truth wins out.
Love never gives up, never loses faith,
is always hopeful, and endures through every circumstance. . . .
Let love be your highest goal.
1 CORINTHIANS 13:4–7, 14:1 (NLT)

Love has nothing to do with what you are expecting to get—only
with what you are expecting to give—which is everything.
—KATHARINE HEPBURN

I would like to have engraved inside every wedding band BE KIND TO ONE ANOTHER. This is the Golden Rule of marriage and the secret of making love last through the years.

—RANDOLPH RAY, *My Little Church Around the Corner*

Love is always open arms. If you close your arms about love, you will find that you are left holding only yourself.

—LEO BUSCAGLIA

The measure of one's devotion is doing, not merely saying. Love is demonstration, not merely saying. Love is demonstration, not merely declaration.

—ANONYMOUS

Between a man and his wife nothing ought to rule but love.

—WILLIAM PENN (1693)

True love's the gift which God has given
To man alone beneath the heaven:
It is not fantasy's hot fire,
Whose wishes, soon as granted, fly;
It liveth not in fierce desire,
With dead desire it doth not die;
It is the secret sympathy,
The silver link, the silken tie,
Which heart to heart and mind to mind
In body and in soul can bind.

—SIR WALTER SCOTT

Love must cease to be a supplement to the real and become reality itself, which it always was. Like a low lovely hum, you must sense it always in the background. Like the soft ringing of bells in the wind, you must feel the sound. Like a heartbeat of the mind, you must always know it is there.

—HUGH & GAYLE PRATHER, *Notes to Each Other*

Yes, marriage is a great risk—it's a plunge into the deep. But the greater the risk we take on God, the deeper and farther we dare to go from the safe shore, the richer shall be the treasures we will find and the greater the delights.

—INGRID TROBISCH, *On Our Way Rejoicing*

Phebe. Good shepherd, tell this youth what 'tis to love.
Silvius. It is to be all made of sighs and tears. . . .
It is to be all made of faith and service. . .
All made of passion and all made of wishes,
All adoration, duty, and observance,
All humbleness, all patience and impatience,
All purity, all trial, all observance;
And so am I for Phebe.
—WILLIAM SHAKESPEARE, *As You Like It*

Because God's love is in me it can come to you from a different and special direction that would be closed if He did not live in me, and because His love is in you it can come to me from a quarter it would not otherwise come. And because it is in both of us, God has greater glory.
—THOMAS MERTON, *New Seeds of Contemplation*

Give thy heart's best treasure,
And the more thou spendest
From thy little store,
With a double bounty,
God will give thee more.
—ADELAIDE A. PROCTOR

Love Letter
from Henry Preston to his wife, Mary, 1934

Dear Mary,

This is an anniversary letter for you (to make up for the lack of gift). I just wanted to tell you how happy I am with you and with our marriage. I know that neither one of us is perfect (I am certainly not!) and yet the two of us together as a unit come much closer to perfection than I ever thought possible.

Some days I hardly see you, I must confess, I've grown so accustomed to your face across the table or beside me on the pillow. (But if you were gone, you'd leave an aching hole in my life that would blot out everything.) Other days, I look at you as though I were seeing you for the first time, and I fall in love all over again with this beautiful and fascinating stranger who shares my life.

I love you, Mary. You have helped me be a better man, I do not doubt, a humbler, gentler, happier man. Most of all, you more than any other have helped me see God's face. Like our heavenly Father, you see my strengths; and you know my private weaknesses. You admire my achievements; and you gaze unflinching at my many faults. Either way, your love for me remains, true and reliable, as mysterious to me as grace. How can I doubt God's love, when He has given me yours?

Thank you, my love. Happy Anniversary.

Dear God, thank You that You have revealed Yourself to us in our love for one another. Once again, we give You our love so that You can fill it to the brim with Your Spirit. May it be a vehicle consecrated to You, so that we may not only touch each other with Your love, but also that we may reach out to those around us.

Thank You for sending Christ to be the model of perfect love. Thank You that our own imperfections and weaknesses really don't matter, because we are relying on Your strength and total perfection. Please continue to bless our love. Amen.

I am giving you a new commandment:
Love each other.
Just as I have loved you,
you should love each other.
Your love for one another will prove
to the world that you are my disciples.
JOHN 13:34 –35 (NLT)